TIME TO GO
~A Journey from Old Deal to New Zealand~

Written and Published by Jerry Vyse

*This book is dedicated to Patrick Hardman, who lives in Mill Hill, Deal.
'Big Pat' served over 27 years for Walmer Lifeboats, during which time
119 lives were saved from shipwreck.*

ISBN:978-0-9563293-0-1
Copyright © Jerry Vyse 2009
www.jerryvyse.com
Printed in England by Mickle Print
www.mickleprint.com

Introduction

150 years ago a group of people from the English town of Deal emigrated to New Zealand, knowing they would probably never return.

Why did they leave? How did they get there? And what happened to them when they arrived?

Born and bred in Deal, I wanted to find answers to these questions. But there are no books written directly about them. So I decided to write one myself.

Cutting from a New Zealand newspaper advertising for descendants of the families who left Deal to share information and help in the creation of this book.

I went to New Zealand and stayed with descendants of the people who left Deal, and other well wishers. I gathered as much information as I could find from anyone that had anything to share, then returned to Deal and finished piecing the story together.

This book is the result, I hope you enjoy it.

Jerry Vyse 2009

CONTENTS

CONTENTS

CHAPTER ONE
DEAL

CHAPTER TWO
THE JOURNEY

CHAPTER THREE
NEW ZEALAND

CHAPTER ONE

DEAL

Deal today is a town of around thirty thousand people, most of whom are friendly.

Aerial view of Deal in 2009.

Over the years many people have fallen in love with Deal. The town has been described as **'delightful'** by the poet John Sparke and **'heavenly'** by the comedian Norman Wisdom.

So why would anyone want to leave the place?

To find out one must go back to long, long ago…

Once upon a time Deal was a very busy place, full of prostitution, alcoholism and gun crime.

Deal had grown rapidly in size in the 1600s due to the increasing amount of large sailing ships travelling past its coastline. They were too big to stop in the shallow harbours at Dover and Sandwich. Instead the ships would anchor in 'The Downs' and wait for favourable winds to continue their journey up towards London or down the English Channel.

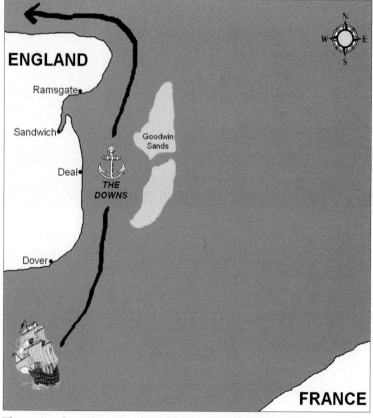

The route of a sailing ship travelling past England's south-east coastline.

To cater for the rise in shipping anchored off Deal's coastline, a class of mariners came into existence known as the 'Deal boatmen'. They would travel out in boats to the anchored sailing ships and offer services, such as taking out supplies, offloading mail or piloting a ship to its next port of call.

Deal boatmen.

A boat being launched from Deal's shingle
beach to give assistance to passing sailing ships.

The Deal boatmen also became famous nationally for rescuing people from ships that had run aground on the Goodwin Sands. The 'Goodwins' is a vast sandbank which when covered with water at high tide becomes quicksand that can completely swallow a ship in days or even hours. The Goodwin Sands has been described as **'one of the most treacherous places in the World'**.[1]

The Goodwin Sands.

By the 1700s Deal was one of the busiest ports in the country, and according to folklore **'there was a pub and a brothel for every day of the year'**.[2] It was not always live and let live though – drinking on Sundays was frowned upon, and if prostitutes were 'caught in the act' they were arrested and publically whipped.

The Ship Inn, one of Deal's old public houses.   *81 Beach Street, once a thriving brothel.*

As the amount of work for the Deal boatmen increased, so did the opportunities to conduct a darker side to their profession – smuggling. For many boatmen their main source of income came from trading alcohol, coffee, tea, wool, silk, gold, silver and other goods tax free in The Downs. They were undeterred by the death penalty for smuggling though it did encourage them to use firearms. Fighting between customs officers and smugglers was sometimes so dangerous that **'the people of Deal were afraid to go out'**,[3] in case they got shot by a stray bullet.

The Deal boatmen's prosperity peaked at the end of the 1700s as they were busy taking out soldiers to the passing Navy ships that were fighting the French. The Times reported that **'the town was so full that the officers are unable to procure beds and sleep upon carpets in the different inns and many of their soldiers on their baggage on the beach'.**[4]

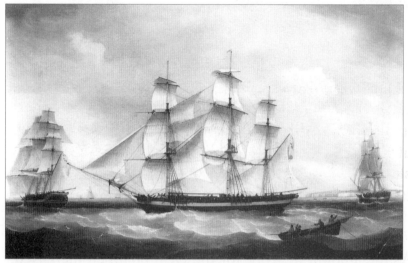

Sailing ships travelling through The Downs during the Napoleonic Wars.

But the long period of peace that followed the end of the wars in 1815 meant there was not as much work for the Deal boatmen. The Royal Navy, with less to do, managed to successfully crack down on smuggling. And the Deal boatmen's income dropped dramatically for their services to ships. Many blamed this on government policies, especially the regulations introduced for piloting.

Deal experienced bleak poverty. Around this time a writer made some not too pleasant remarks about the town: **'Deal is a most villainous place...full of filthy looking people...everything seems upon the perish...I was glad to hurry along through it and leave its inns and public houses to be occupied by the tarred, and trowsered, and blue and buff crew whose very vicinage I always detest.'**[5]

The most serious threat to the Deal boatmen's work came from the growing use of steam power. Almost all the shipped mail bags that used to be offloaded at Deal were instead being taken to Plymouth and Southampton and transported by steam train. Steam tugboats berthed at Ramsgate and Dover could supply or rescue sailing ships much quicker than a boat from Deal. And the new large steam ships could travel independently of wind and current. This meant they did not need to anchor in The Downs and were far less likely to drift into the Goodwin Sands.

Deal boatmen waiting for work.

By the 1850s the once busy, prosperous boatmen were going weeks without work. And there were no obvious solutions to solving their unemployment. The Royal Navy had strict age and height restrictions for people that wanted to join. Those that did get in had to fork out a large amount of money just for their uniform - hardly ideal for people living in poverty. There was also great animosity in Deal about the Navy as many Deal boatmen had volunteered during the wars with the French but got no pension payouts.

Fishing was not a suitable option either. The amount of shipping in The Downs made the risk of damage to nets unacceptably high. For those that did fish, the summer mackerel season was a short one and had failed more than once in the 1850s. At other times of the year catches were being left to rot on the beach because the price obtainable was so low.

Not everyone sympathized with the Deal boatmen's poverty. A letter in the local newspaper moaned about them **'smoking, spitting and giving audible utterance to such language which every decent person must revolt at'.**[6] Deal was being pushed as a holiday destination around this point, and one tourist wrote: **'it is hardly fair that visitors should be compelled to submit to the constant annoyance of a set of idle men who are allowed to smoke and spit without the least possible restraint...the language too frequently used is most abominable and disgusting.'**[7]

Luckily for the boatmen the problems they faced were recognised by some wealthy people that were in a position to help. In September 1858 a meeting was held at Deal Town Hall. Billed as a **'Mariners Tea Party'**[8] the gathering was more than just a social event. It found a solution that would change a handful of the boatmen's lives forever – **emigration**.

Deal Town Hall

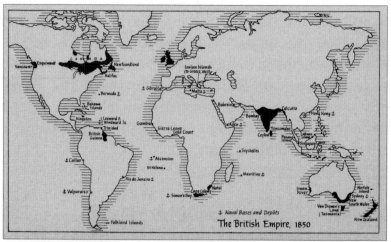

Map highlighting the extent of the British Empire in the 1850s.

In the previous fifteen years it is estimated that over three million people had emigrated from Britain to the colonies. Most went to North America, though going 'down under' was becoming increasingly popular. An emigration officer that had just returned from Australia said he would be happy to help the unemployed youngsters from Deal emigrate as there were more jobs for them overseas.

The meeting ended on friendly terms, sweetened further by the tobacco the boatmen had been given to take home with them.

Less than three weeks later another meeting was held. The main speaker was James Fitzgerald. He was the Emigration Secretary at the time, overseeing those who left Britain on ships to the colonies. One of these countries was New Zealand, from where Fitzgerald had recently returned. New Zealand had joined the British Empire less than twenty years before. The population of the country around that time was only about eighty thousand. Almost all of the inhabitants lived on the North Island and were mainly 'Maoris'.[9]

Fitzgerald had been the first Superintendant of a province called 'Canterbury' on the South Island. The first significant number of British settlers began arriving in this area in the 1850s. An almost endless supply of jobs awaited the new arrivals. Fitzgerald was well aware of this when he returned to Britain to become Emigration Secretary.

James Fitzgerald.

By attending the meeting it would appear Fitzgerald was putting two and two together – underemployment in Canterbury coupled with unemployment in Deal. But it went deeper than simple mathematics. In one letter Fitzgerald remarked that the Deal boatmen were **'not the men most wanted in Canterbury'**.[10] At that time there were strict controls over who was allowed to emigrate. Much preferred were tradesmen and farm labourers (though ten years later these rules were so relaxed that one emigrant ship had four London prostitutes on board).

The real reason Fitzgerald had come to Deal to help the boatmen was a personal attachment he had to them since his youth. At the meeting he remarked: **'I spent much of my boyhood days among them and am therefore thoroughly acquainted with their habits and bravery.'**[11] And so Fitzgerald decided to use his position of power to fund the emigration of six Deal boatmen and their families on a ship called the *Mystery*, which was due to leave for the South Island of New Zealand in December 1858.

He believed this decision would be supported by the general public, later writing: **'I thought it right to come forward to aid in a charitable work which considering the romance which rests around the character of the boatmen of Deal has a national importance.'**[12] He reckoned the boatmen would be able to establish a fishery out there, though he gave them **'no promises of any** kind'.[13]

A poster encouraging people to emigrate to the colonies

By the end of the meeting an agreement had been fixed. Older boatmen were to remain in Deal to continue their profession, whilst younger boatmen with wives would be encouraged to emigrate to New Zealand. Six families funded by the Government, and any others that could raise the money would have the right to emigrate too.

The six Government-funded boatmen chosen were:

ROBERT BOWBYES, **27**, and his wife Harriet, 22.
JOHN BOWLES, **39**, his wife Elizabeth, 30, *two daughters.*
HENRY CLAYSON, **22**, his wife Elizabeth, 20, *one son.*
MORRIS CORY, **29**, his wife Elizabeth, 29, *two sons and two daughters.*
WILLIAM ROBERTS, **21**, and his wife Harriet, 19.
JOHN WILDS, 32, and his wife Esther, 26.

Silver Street, where Morris Cory grew up. He was to leave behind a large number of relatives in Deal - his family had lived in the town for many generations.

19

In the following weeks a further seven boatmen managed to stump up enough cash for the emigration of themselves and their families. They were:

JOHN GARDNER, **28**, his wife Sibylla, 24,
one son and one daughter.
NEAME HAYWARD, **35**, his wife Susan, 30,
two sons.
EDWARD NEWTON, **32**, his wife Sarah, 27,
three sons.
JOHN NEWTON, 32, his wife Jane, 32,
two sons and two daughters.
RICHARD NORRIS, 28, his wife Emma, 24,
one daughter.
RICHARD ROGERS, 38, his wife Charlotte, 29,
three sons and two daughters.
THOMAS WYMAN, 43, his wife Jane, 42,
three sons and four daughters.

Hence, there were thirteen boatmen due to emigrate to New Zealand on the *Mystery*: **six Government-funded** and **seven self-funded**, which with their families totalled fifty-eight people in all.

The emigrating boatmen were donated a lugger (a type of boat that was popular in Deal) called the *Fox* and were permitted to take it with them on the ship. It was fitted with all the fishing equipment it was anticipated they would need including trails, nets and oyster dredges.

The emigrants were also given £50 to share between them from the 'Deal Committee', which had been set up to raise money for schemes that would assist Deal boatmen. Donations had come in from all over the country after a long pleading letter was published in The Times explaining why the boatmen were living in dire poverty.

In December 1858 the thirteen Deal boatmen and their families said farewell to the town they had once called home. They boarded the *Mystery* at Charing Cross, London. Destination: New Zealand.

Middle Street, which runs through the main residential area of old Deal. The foundations of many of the houses date back to the 1600s. The emigrating boatmen and their families knew that once they boarded the ship they would probably not walk along Deal's narrow streets and alleyways ever again.

CHAPTER TWO
THE JOURNEY

Over fifty emigrant ships set sail from Britain to New Zealand in 1858. The journey usually took over three months.

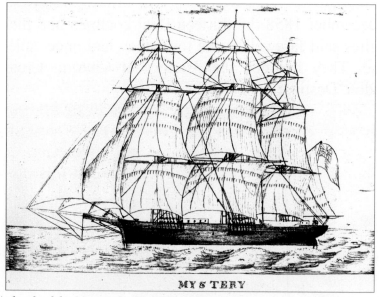

A sketch of the Mystery by Malcolm Millar, a shepherd travelling on board. The ship weighed over a thousand tons.

The *Mystery* was making its first voyage of this kind, and was under the command of Captain Matthews. Although the captains chosen had great skill to control a ship for such a long trip, they were not always sensible. After the death of a woman on a ship that had sailed a year before, the captain **'was so much concerned that he was drunk for about a week afterwards'**.[15]

The crew consisted of numerous sailors, two stewards, four cooks, a doctor and a schoolmaster. There were four constables and a matron on board – these were usually selected from among the emigrants and paid a small allowance. Also boarding the ship were pigs, sheep and chicken. Pets comprised of three dogs, two monkeys and a cat.[16] The ship was carrying cargo too, including crates of perfume, a ten ton bridge and three turnip cutters.[17]

There were around 320 people on board from opposite parts of the country and different walks of life. From a 21 year-old Dundee ploughman to a middle-aged carpenter from Cornwall travelling with his wife and five children. There was also a couple from Germany on board. Many of the women, including at least three of the Deal boatmen's wives, were pregnant.

Boarding the ship.

Each passenger was allocated space on the ship for baggage. It was recommended they brought a good supply of clothing. They also needed other items, such as a mattress, sheets, a washing bowl and a tea pot.

The teapot which the Wilds family brought with them from Deal.

The *Mystery* had on board a large amount of general goods, enough to feed and take care of the passengers for the whole of their journey. Food and drink included salted beef, salted pork, rice, peas, potatoes, biscuits, tea, coffee and an array of alcoholic beverages. Alcohol would only ever be given out for **'medicinal purposes'**, though this rule was usually flouted.[18]

The cabin (first class) passengers had their own rooms and were served their meals by one of the stewards. They also had the best area of deck for private relaxation. They rarely mixed with the steerage (second class) passengers. These made up the bulk of the population on board and included the Deal boatmen.

The steerage passengers lived in a vast hall below the deck. Despite regulations the general policy was to pack as many people in as possible to save costs. One person described this area as having a **'pestilential atmosphere created by the festering mass of squalid humanity imprisoned between the damp and steaming decks...the miseries of filth, foul air and darkness...hundreds of men, women and children, dressing and undressing, washing, quarrelling, fighting, cooking and drinking.'**[19]

After leaving London the ship docked at Gravesend, a popular stop off point where supplies were picked up and passengers had a last chance to go ashore. Some families were landed here after symptoms of small pox were discovered. Scarlett fever was also spreading fast, especially amongst the children. By the time the *Mystery* was in The Downs, help was being called for from Deal. Neame Hayward acted as a messenger.[20]

The sea doctor attempting to contain diseases.

After being anchored for several days the *Mystery* continued on its voyage. All the Deal families survived the journey, although the early diseases had not been sufficiently contained. A total of fifteen children died. They were aged between 1 and 5 years and most had died of small pox. Funerals were usually conducted the same day by holding the baby off the edge of the ship on a plank. One description of a shipboard funeral reads: **'This morning at six o'clock the child was sewn in a piece of canvas with a cannon ball at the feet. It was dropped from the board into the sea. The sea doctor read the burial service.'** On that same ship a few days after a burial at sea a shark was caught by the sailors and eaten by the passengers. The sailors neglected to tell them that **'in the large shark yesterday that was caught was found a child's leg'**.[21]

The sailors were given a flat fee for the journey, so to get to New Zealand as quickly as possible the *Mystery* did not stop once after leaving Britain. This was also to avoid ship desertions. Sea sickness usually broke out for the first few weeks. The weather tended to get calmer by the South Atlantic before westerly winds sped ships up on the last leg. To navigate the ship a sextant was used at midday to measure the angle of the sun. This could then be used to calculate the latitude. They measured the speed of the ship by dropping a piece of wood of the ship with a fine piece of line knotted at intervals.

A sailor climbing up the rigging of the ship.

The sailors had a mixed relationship with the passengers. One description of a sailor asserts that he was **'most profane, or rather blasphemous, especially if any of the passengers made any litter on the deck'**. The diarist depicts another sailor as **'more detached, but just as direct, his language might be described as a profanity pump...it ran in such an easy stream'**.[22]

There were numerous rules and duties on board the ship for the passengers. They had both a bed time and a time to wake up. They were required to clean the ship regularly. There were clothes washing duties for the women, whilst men in turn were required to keep order at night and help any sick people. The Deal boatman John Bowles wrote in a letter home that **'there was a great deal of sickness in the ship all the way out'**, though the Deal children were **'well and hearty'**.[23] Bowles ended up being a witness in the trial of a man convicted of thieving alcohol on board. Various ales and a cask of gin had been found empty in the store room.[24]

Scrubbing the deck clean.

Hygiene was often a cause for concern. Maggots were frequently found in the food, and every ship had its fair share of rats. A report on an emigrant ship states that **'it appeared never, since the ship leaving London, to have been swept or cleaned in any way. There was** one mass of filth and rubbish from which arose a stench which at times must have been unbearable'.[25] This was a concern to one emigrant, who wrote: 'turned the Mrs out of bed and made her have a good wash all over with sea water. Mean to do so every morning.' Incidentally, upon arrival he states that his wife is 'quite fat and saucy'.[26]

There were plenty of dangers faced at sea. Just three years earlier the *Guilding Star* had left Liverpool with over 500 emigrants on board, never to be seen again. And although the majority of the ships made it to their destinations, it was inevitable they would face stormy seas. One emigrant described how during a rough day the ship was rocking 'to and fro like a drunk man...water cans, pots and pans tumbling in all directions'.[27]

The second class passengers, living below the deck, faced a difficult situation. If they opened the hatchway, water would pour in. But if it was closed then they would be in complete darkness.

Stormy seas.

There are many seedy tales of behaviour between the crew and the single women on emigrant ships. Some occurrences were documented by the Deputy Immigration Officer: **'There were three girls in the pantry with the steward. One girl named Shepherd had her arms around his neck, both being then in a standing position.'** He also reported an event involving **'about twelve couples – men, girls and sailors, some in a reclining position, others half reclining and a few sitting all huddled together with arms thrown around each others necks'**. They were making **'unmistakable sounds'**.[28]

The single women were meant to be monitored by the matron, but she often turned a blind eye. One diarist noted an incident where a woman **'went completely mad and tore all her clothes off'**. On another occasion **'the captain found one of the quartermasters drunk with a single girl'**.[29] In an attempt to stop this **'disgraceful conduct'** the Deputy Immigration Officer recommended that the single women should be supplied with books and knitting materials. This, it was believed, would **'in a measure occupy the minds of the girls'**.[30]

Women knitting on the top deck.

Despite the cramped conditions, the Deal couples still found intimate time. Richard and Emma Norris conceived their daughter Mary on board.

Besides cooking, cleaning, knitting and satisfying carnal desires, there were other ways the emigrants kept themselves entertained. Contests were held in walking, jumping and wrestling. Dominoes, cards and board games were popular. Some people grouped together to sing songs. There were opportunities to dance, though the single men and women needed the permission of the Captain. As was customary at the time, the emigrants were encouraged to read the bible. There was also the natural entertainment available of watching out for birds, fish and other sailing ships.

Men looking at birds.

In March 1859 the *Mystery* arrived at Lyttelton Harbour, New Zealand. The ship had taken over eighty days to reach its destination. At the time this was considered to be a very quick passage. A British author who arrived in New Zealand that year wrote: **'The World begins to feel very small when one finds one can get halfway round it in three months.'**[31]

The entrance to Lyttelton Harbour.

CHAPTER THREE
NEW ZEALAND

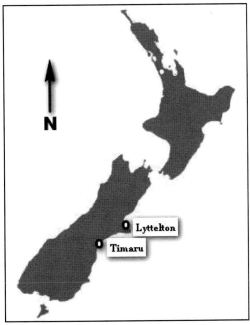

Map of New Zealand showing the locations of
Lyttelton and Timaru.

LYTTELTON

When the *Mystery* arrived in Lyttelton it was put into quarantine but no contamination was found to remain. Equally no reoccurring symptoms were found in the passengers, so they were let off. Many people were provisionally housed in the nearby barracks, including the families from Deal.

A sketch of Lyttelton in the 1850s.

The Deal boatmen immediately proved their worth by successfully unloading the ship. As a result, the self-funded boatmen got employment at Lyttelton Harbour on small boats loading and unloading goods and people from the ships anchored in the port. One report states they were **'setting an example to the old hands'** and in the process earning a decent wage.[32] They were so busy that they did not have the time to conduct their fishing venture until a couple of years later.

Neame Hayward died within a year of being in New Zealand. News of his early death found its way back to Deal and was reported in the Deal Telegram, the local paper at the time. There were, though, more positive reports sent back to their hometown. One letter posted home reads: **'We have found the place better than expected. The country looks beautiful.'**[33] No doubt these positive reports helped encourage further emigration from Deal to New Zealand – there were several Deal families that travelled out on the *Regina* in 1859, though not with government assistance. This was, though, the last emigrant ship to New Zealand with a significant number of Deal boatmen on board.[34]

Lyttelton Harbour in the 1860s.

The fishery was finally established in Lyttelton by the self-funded boatmen in 1861. Kick started with a £60 investment from the Provincial Government, their attempts at offshore fishing ended in disaster. After two years they were registered as bankrupt. They would have been forced to sell the Deal lugger they had brought with them.

It is not surprising that they failed - fishing was not a familiar occupation for many Deal boatmen, and it would have been even more difficult to fish in untried and deeper waters. Any fish they did catch would rarely have reached a decent price because the price of other foods, especially lamb, was usually very low.

So what became of the self-funded Deal boatmen?

Richard Rogers became a bootmaker and then a labourer. He died in Lyttelton of dysentery aged 56. This was a sad irony considering he had been charged several years previous for infecting a public well with chloride of lime.[35] Richard lived just long enough to see his eldest daughter marry and have her first child. Richard's widowed wife Charlotte became a launderer, remarried and died at the age of 72 in Dunedin.

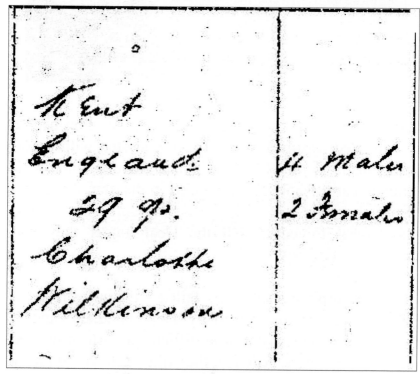

Part of Richard's death certificate

John Gardner died in Lyttelton aged 70, having spent all of his life working on boats. Two months later his widowed wife Sibylla committed suicide. The *Lyttelton Times* stated she **'was missing from the cottage in which she was living alone...During the day a letter was found in the house in which she stated her intention of doing away with herself, and about 7.30pm that day her body was found by Constable McCormack and others on the rocks below Long Point. She had evidently fallen over the cliff which at the place is about eighty feet in height and the remains were in a terribly battered condition.'**[36]

John and Sibylla photographed together.

Edward Newton moved south to Timaru and became a fisherman. Police records suggest his wife Sarah sought a protection order against him in addition to custody of their children, although both cases were later withdrawn.[37] After suffering two serious accidents Edward moved to Gisborne, where he died aged 87.

Thomas Wyman became a fruit and veg seller to ships, as well as establishing a boat service to take people between Diamond Harbour and Lyttelton. Thomas had many more children with his wife Jane. When he died in Lyttelton aged 91 he had outlived some of them. He left behind three sons, three daughters, forty-six grandchildren and thirty-seven great grandchildren. His Deal-born daughter Fanny had an illegitimate child, baptized privately in Lyttelton.[38]

Waterman's Cottage in Diamond Harbour, which for years was used by Thomas Wyman to conduct his work.

John Newton died at the ripe old age of 93. He entered the public service before returning to the sea as a boatman employed by the Lyttelton Harbour Board. He retired at the age of 75. Like many of the other Deal boatmen that emigrated he had a large family - when he died he left behind five sons, two daughters, twenty-eight grandchildren and forty-five great grandchildren.[39]

Richard Norris gained a reputation in Lyttelton for his eccentricity. He was nicknamed *'Bagowinckel Dick'*, apparently for his skills in making rigging for sailing ships. Sometimes when he saw young cyclists he would poke his walking stick into their front wheel.

A cartoon satirising the eccentric Richard Norris.

One day his wife Emma asked him to go out and buy some butter and he did not return for many months. He had boarded a ship. His wife was not too pleased. Not only did his illiteracy mean that he did not send her any letters to tell her where he had gone, but when he returned he did not have any butter.

Emma died at the age of 61. Richard became an alcoholic, joined the Salvation Army to preach against drinking, only to return to alcoholism. This cycle repeated itself many times.[40]

Richard Norris in his Salvation Army days.

Despite his boozing, it is stated on Richard's gravestone that he lived til he was 94. Other reports suggest he died between the age of 85 and 92. He left behind thirty-four grandchildren and sixteen great grandchildren.

His Deal-born daughter Sarah moved out of Lyttelton to the more rural Owen Valley. She died aged 88.

Sarah Norris in later life.

TIMARU

The six government-funded boatmen worked for several weeks as signalmen in Lyttelton before more suitable work was found for them a hundred miles south in a place called Timaru.

Sketch of Timaru in the 1850s.

One literal translation of Timaru from Maori to English is **'shady cabbage tree'**. However, **'place of shelter'** is a more fitting and less odd interpretation of the name.[41] From the earliest known times Timaru was a place of shelter for Maori canoes moving up and down the coast. But there were almost no permanent inhabitants.

In 1859 an entrepreneur called Henry LeCren established a landing service at Timaru so that wool could be shipped to Lyttelton and beyond. The men manning the landing boats tended to be ship deserters, often drunkards, who rarely stayed long in Timaru. A culture of **'ruffianism'** was apparently present in a workforce that was a **'very lawless mob of runaway sailors'**.[42]

So LeCren decided to take on the more permanent and professional Deal boatmen. They travelled the hazardous hundred mile journey overland and got straight to work as soon as they arrived. Their principal job was to load and unload goods and people onto the ships anchored off shore. The landing service initially used whaleboats before switching to wooden surf boats. These were drawn on skids by a capstan and cable so were familiar to the boatmen. Working hours tended to be long as they were required to keep going until the job was done. This often meant they did not finish until midnight. They sometimes had the assistance of a Scotsman named 'Strong Work Morrison' as coxswain.

Operating the landing service.

It did not take long for them to prove their talent. For a ship called the *Spray* the boatmen manage to unload forty thousand feet of timber and forty tons of goods followed by loading on over two hundred bales of wool - all in just three days. Apparently this would have taken Timaru's previous inhabitants between seven and thirteen days. One newspaper reported that **'the state of things differs remarkably from that which prevailed some few months ago…LeCren deserves thanks for having been the means of introducing the Deal boatmen into a business which suits them so exactly'**.[43]

But it was not just in their profession that the Deal boatmen earned respect. They voluntarily carried all the timber for the erection of a new Church in the town. Had they been paid to do this they would each have received £4. This would have been equivalent to a month's wages – the boatmen were earning £50 a year at the landing service. Back then that was considered decent pay, especially taking into account what the boatmen had left behind.

They still acted with financial restraint. John Bowles stated in a letter home that he was saving his money by not going into the pubs. Evidence suggests that they did manage to keep away from the 'grog shops'. One report stated that they were **'civil, industrious and not given to drink'**.[44] This is relative to the previous workers, so it is likely the boatmen still enjoyed the occasional pint.

The boatmen built six cottages on an acre of land sold cheaply to them by LeCren. At that time there were only fourteen other cottages in Timaru. A short walk inland from the coast along a sheep track, the area became known as 'Dealtown'. They named the road they lived on 'Middle Street', after its namesake in Deal. To get water they had to go to a well near the Police Station. One notable home was built by William Roberts. The walls were eighteen inches thick and made of cob – a mixture of sand, clay, straw, water and earth.

The cob cottage built by William Roberts. For over a hundred years it stayed in the hands of Deal descendants, passed on to the Baker family who kept it in the same condition. It was demolished in the 1960s after the last Baker inhabitant died and the council refused to purchase it.

Less than a year after they had arrived in Timaru Henry Clayson drowned after his boat capsized when he was attempting to land. Many Deal boatmen could not swim, which proved fatal for Clayson.

The Deal boatmen became a team of six once more when they were joined by Phillip Foster, who had travelled out from Deal on the *Regina*. But it was not long before another tragic incident occurred involving Bowbyes, Bowles, Cory, Foster and Roberts.

A ship had been anchored off the coast of Timaru after narrowly escaping a wreck. It was stuck in a strong gale. The crew were still on board, and the Deal boatmen watched out for the ship night and day in case they needed assistance. They burnt lights on the shore to remind those on board they were still on the lookout.

When they sighted the ship's crew working on the anchorage, they believed the ship must be in distress.

A storm hits Timaru.

They were unable to launch their lifeboat, so they went out in a small two-oared boat. But the sea was far too rough and **'a huge wave capsized them'**. They all ended up in the water.

Roberts was carried to shore by some large waves and survived fully intact. Bowles too was dashed up by the waves, and despite being **'severely beaten'** he lived to tell the tale. Foster clung to the overturned boat for almost an hour before he was **'washed off and cast alive on shore'**. The other two boatmen were not so lucky. Cory drowned almost immediately. And Bowbyes **'clung to an oar for some time, but drowned from exhaustion'**. Although a shocking event, the two that died have been remembered as heroes. Despite travelling to the other side of the World they had not lost their willingness to save lives in stormy seas.[45]

Landing services continued for twenty years until they became unnecessary. A railway line had been built through Timaru – passengers wishing to go there could disembark at Lyttelton and take the train, and cargo could be transported by rail. A harbour was then constructed at Timaru, so any ships wishing to unload goods or people could do so by mooring in the breakwater.

So what became of the Government-funded Deal boatmen?

Henry Clayson as stated drowned shortly after his arrival. He was 27. Widowed Elizabeth, who had two children to fend for, married William Wood and had a further three. They went back to Deal in 1865, presumably so the new children and husband could meet Elizabeth's parents and siblings (Elizabeth was one of fourteen children). After several months back in Deal they boarded the *London* to return to New Zealand. Tragically the ship hit a storm in the Bay of Biscay and Elizabeth, William and all the children drowned. One survivor witnessed Elizabeth drown: **'When I last saw Mrs Wood she was standing up to her armpits in water with the baby in her arms. It was a pitiful thing to see. I took a flask from my pocket which was half full of Brandy and gave her a sip to revive her, but she said it was too late as her husband and four other children had already drowned and she wanted to go with them. She asked me to save the baby but it was too late as she collapsed with the baby in her arms, and was gone.'**[46]

Morris Cory, who was washed ashore at Timaru from the fatal rescue mission, is buried in the local cemetery. His widowed wife Elizabeth paid for his gravestone, which was the first to be laid there. How she afforded this is unknown, though a fund was set up to help the widows and orphans of the drowned boatmen.[47] Elizabeth never remarried and when she died at the age of 85 she was reunited with Morris.

IN LOVING MEMORY OF
MORRIS CLAYSON CORY,
DROWNED OFF TIMARU,
OCTOBER 6TH 1860,
AGED 30 YEARS.

———

IN THE MIDST OF LIFE WE ARE IN DEATH.

ALSO
ELIZABETH THOMPSON,
WIFE OF THE ABOVE
WHO DIED MARCH 20TH 1913,
AGED 85 YEARS.

REUNITED AFTER MANY YEARS.

Morris and Elizabeth's gravestone, the first to be laid in Timaru cemetery, is kept clean by their great grandson Roy Clarkson.

William Bowbyes, who also died in the notorious rescue mission, can be found at Timaru Cemetery. However, his wife Harriet did not pay for a gravestone, so he is buried in what is known as the 'pauper' section. Harriet remarried the following year and they moved south to the province of Otago. She died in a town called Roxburgh at the age of 93.

William Roberts died aged 29 of tuberculosis, leaving two children fatherless. His widowed wife Harriet found another man, but he died when she was pregnant. Finally she found a husband with longevity. Harriet married a man called Sylvester Passmore. For a time his job in Timaru was a 'town scavenger' – this meant he had to collect all the local human excrement. They had six children together. Harriet died at the age of 61 and Sylvester joined her two weeks later.

Sylvester and Harriet photographed together.

John Bowles moved to the nearby village of Waimate where he became a farmer. He was elected to a committee to start a school, and donated £3. He died aged 56. On his tombstone it states: **'the finger of the Lord touched him while he slept'**. The epitaph sounds fitting as the local newspaper reported that on the night he died **'he awoke and complained of feeling very cold and almost immediately expired'**.[48] His widowed wife Elizabeth remarried two years later. Bizarrely it was to the older brother of the man who had married her daughter a fortnight before.[49] Elizabeth died aged 82.

John Wilds became a farmer and a market gardener. His wife Esther had been a teacher in Deal, and continued her profession in Timaru. At the age of 69 she drowned in the water of a nearby dam. Her husband had the unpleasant experience of sighting her: **'he walked down the garden and on coming to the dam...was horrified to see the body of his wife floating in the water.'**[50] With the help of his son and a neighbour they pulled her out and sent for a doctor, but it was too late. She was **'beyond medical aid'**. An inquest was held and a verdict of accidental drowning was given. The jury concluded that Esther must have fallen down the slippery slopes, where she often went to collect eggs.[51]

Following her death John's health slowly deteriorated, both physically and mentally. One report states that **'his mind was wandering'**[52] - a subtle way of saying that he was suffering from depression.

At the age of 88 John had a painful operation that would have left most people unable to walk. However, early the next day he wandered down to the beach and walked into the sea. A worker at the harbour pulled him out alive and sent him home in a taxi cab. Later that morning his son went round to his house. **'The old man, who was really in his dotage, told his son that he was feeling very well, but that he had been down to the sea to drown himself that morning.'**[53]

The son went to work, thinking his father must have dreamt it. John again went down to the sea, but this time when he was heaved out it was too late. The sudden immersion in cold water had caused his heart to stop beating.

John and Esther Wilds (sat in the middle)
with their six children.

Conclusion

It was deep rooted poverty that had driven the Deal families to do whatever they could to improve the state of their lives and give their children a brighter future. The possibility of work and happiness in a faraway land was strong enough to lure them away from their friends and relatives in Deal, knowing they may never see them again.

After a long journey they arrived at their destination. As immigrants they gave to New Zealand their boating skills, a hard-work ethic and a pinch of eccentricity. All these things appear to have been beneficial to the country.

Most of the boatmen had large families, which means today there are literally hundreds of people in New Zealand that descend from the men and women that left Deal 150 years ago. Many no longer live in the same towns that their ancestors inhabited, most no longer have the same surnames, and probably all of them now have a New Zealand accent.

But it could be said that in one way their Deal roots are not forgotten. The descendants I met did not hesitate to provide me with a bed for the night (or week). Fitting considering the motto on Deal's coat of arms is **'befriend the stranger'**.

The author with descendants of the boatmen at Deal Street, Timaru.
The street is a tribute to the impact the boatmen had in the town.
Timaru today has a population of around thirty thousand.

$\mathcal{F}$ootnotes

[1]*The Times,*26 October, 1866.
[2]Another folklore on this matter is that 'every other house in Deal was a pub or a brothel'. Both of these statements are not far from the truth.
[3]Stuart G. Smith, *Deal: A Brief History*, p.21.
[4]T.J. Sharp *How does the Times Illustrate...*p.4.
[5]William Cobbett, *Rural Rides*, p.203.
[6]*Deal Telegram*, 6 April, 1859.
[7]*Deal Telegram*, 8 August, 1863.
[8]Reports on the meetings were documented in the Deal Telegram, 1858.
[9]*Statistics New Zealand.* There would also have been a handful of early European settlers and some 'Morioris'. It is believed that Maoris and Morioris originated from islands in the Pacific Ocean. Historians disagree over what date they arrived and which tribes arrived first.
[10]Fitzgerald *to Provincial Secretary*, 11 December, Archives New Zealand (ICPS 112/1859).
[11]*Deal Telegram*, 6 October, 1858.
[12]Fitzgerald *to Provincial Secretary*, 11 December, Archives New Zealand (ICPS 112/1859).
[13]Fitzgerald *to Provincial Secretary*, 11 December, Archives New Zealand (ICPS 112/1859).
[14]*Timaru Herald*, 29 December, 1865.
[15]Diary of Agnes Archibald onboard the *Strathallan*, 1857, http://www.rootsweb.ancestry.com
[16]Two week diary of William Johnson on board the *Mystery*, Canterbury Museum.
[17]*Lyttelton Times*, 21-25 February, 1859.
[18]Alan McKenzie, *Timaru at Last!*, p.44.
[19]*The Times*, 14 January, 1854.
[20]*Fitzgerald's Correspondence,* December 1858, Archives New Zealand (CP 596D). John Newton and his family were among those landed. They were treated and ended up sailing on the next emigrant ship, the *Victory.*
[21]James Groves, *The Echunga Diaries: London to New Zealand by Sailing Ship*, p.23.
[22]Diary of Agnes Archibald onboard the *Strathallan*, 1857, http://www.rootsweb.ancestry.com
[23]John Bowles to *William Stanton*, April 30, 1859. Deal Library.
[24]P.J. Pascall, *The Deal Boatmen*, p.3.
[25]Seager *to Provincial Secretary*, 26 July 1859, Archives New Zealand (ICPS 447/1859).
[26]Diary of Arthur Price onboard the *Lancashire Witch*, 1863, http://www.rootsweb.ancestry.com
[27]Diary of a passenger on the *Jura, Timaru Herald*, 9 December, 2008.
[28]Seager *to Provincial Secretary*, 26 July 1859, Archives New Zealand (ICPS 447/1859).
[29]Diary of Arthur Price onboard the *Lancashire Witch*, 1863, http://www.rootsweb.ancestry.com
[30]Seager *to Provincial Secretary*, 26 July 1859, Archives New Zealand (ICPS 447/1859).
[31]Diary of Samuel Butler onboard the *Roman Emperor*, 1860, http://www.yesteryears.co.nz
[32]Provincial Secretary *to Fitzgerald*, 2 May 1859, Archives New Zealand (CP596d/9).
[33]*Deal Telegram*, 30 Nov, 1859.
[34]*The Regina* left in August 1859. The Deal families included Snoswell, Moss, White and Foster.
[35]*Lyttelton Times*, April 9, 1870.
[36]*Lyttelton Times*, 16 January, 1899.
[37]*Timaru Criminal Cases Index, IDs* 7381-7386, South Canterbury Museum.
[38]Chistchurch Library Church Records (HTL2/1446)
[39]E.C. Pain, *Last of Our* Luggers, p.128
[40]Information courtesy of Baden and Ron Norris.
[41]J.B. Hamilton, *The Streets of Timaru*, p.1.
[42]Hamilton and *Provincial Secretary*, March 1859, Archives New Zealand (ICPS 148/1859)
[43]*Otago Witness*, 8 October 1859.
[44]*Deal Telegram*, 30 November, 1859.
[45]John Laker, *The History of Deal*, p.198.
[46]A.J. Smith *The Sorrow of the Sea: A narrative of the shipwreck London*, p.31.
[47]*Lyttelton Times*, 31 October, 1860.
[48]*Timaru Herald*, 21 September, 1867.
[49]*Timaru Herald*, 24 November, 1869.
[50]*Timaru Herald*, 13 November, 1894.
[51]*Timaru Herald*, 14 November, 1894.
[52]E.C. Pain, *Last of Our* Luggers, p.131.
[53]*Timaru Herald*, 21 October, 1912.

Pictures

Bibliography

Deal
George Bethel Bayley *Seamen of the Downs*
Jacqueline Bower *A Traditional Community in Decline*
David Chamberlain *Lost and Found*
William Cobbett *Rural Rides*
Charles Elvin *Records of Walmer*
Beryl Foley-Fisher *Bygone Deal and Walmer*
Ivan Green *The Book of Deal and Walmer*
Gregory Holyoake *Deal: Sad Smuggling Town*
Gregory Holyoake *Deal: All in the Downs*
Lawrence James *The Rise and Fall of the British Empire.*
John Laker *The History of Deal*
Gertrude Nunns *A History of Deal*
E.C. Pain *Last of Our Luggers*
Stephen Pritchard *The History of Deal*
John Lewis Roget *Sketches of Deal, Walmer and Sandwich*
T.J. Sharp *How does the Times Illustrate the History,
Importance, and Position of Deal 1790-1815?* (essay)
Stuart G. Smith *Deal: A Brief History*
William Stanton *Journal of a Deal pilot*
Rev. T.S. Treanor *Heroes of the Goodwin Sands*

Newspapers - Deal Telegram, Deal Mercury, The Times.

Other Sources - Census Records (held at Deal Library).

The Journey / New Zealand
Colin Amodeo *The Mosquito Fleet of Canterbury*
Johannas C. Anderson *Place-names of Banks Peninsula*
Oliver A. Gillespie *South Canterbury: A Record of Settlement*
James Groves *The Echunga Diaries: London to New Zealand by Sailing Ship*.
J.B. Hamilton *The Streets of Timaru*
Charles E. Hassall *A short history of the port of Timaru, 1852-1955*
Alan Mckenzie *Timaru at Last!*
P.J. Pascall *The Deal Boatmen* (essay)
Alistair Pike *Timaru's Boatmen 1852—1886*
A.J. Smith *The Sorrow of the Sea: A narrative of the shipwreck London*
Mary Stapleton-Smith *Diamond Harbour*

Newspapers - Lyttelton Times, Otago Witness and Timaru Herald.

Websites - http://www.paperspast.co.nz
            http://www.yesteryears.co.nz
            http://www.rootsweb.ancestry.com

Other sources - Original letters (held at Archives New Zealand, Christchurch). Church Records (held at Christchurch Library and South Canterbury Museum). Timaru Criminal Cases (held at South Canterbury Museum). Material also received from family collections.

Acknowledgements

This book would not have been possible without the people that have supported me along the way in both Deal and New Zealand.

Deal
Many thanks to the staff who helped at Deal Library and Deal Maritime and Local History Museum.

Special thanks to David Chamberlain, Andrew Chambers, Harold and Claire Chapman, Bert Curling, John and Audrey Downes, Beth Easton, John Ellis, Christine Finn, Frances Fyfield, Steve Glover, Ant Hardman, Gregory Holyoake, Paige Macmillan, Guy Scantlebury, Claire O'Shea, Danny Rhodes, Stuart Smith, Cynthia Tucker, Sheila Vyse, Maurice Walsh.

New Zealand
Many thanks to the staff who helped at Alexander Turnbull Library, Archives New Zealand, Canterbury Museum, Christchurch Library, Lyttelton Museum, South Canterbury Museum and Timaru Library.

Special thanks to Colin Amodeo, Roy Clarkson, Craig and Iona Double, Elizabeth Gazzard, Richard Greenaway, Rona Hayles, Robin and Judy Holdsworth, Phillip Howe, Yvonne Jordan, Alistair Lester, Dave Lester, Gertrude Lester, Alan McKenzie, Rachel Morris, Mark Napier, Baden Norris, Ron Norris, Win Parkes, Peter Pascall, Alistair Pike, Tony Rippin, Ross Sellwood, Ralph and Valarie Ritchie, John and Pat Sutherland, Heather Weir, Malcolm and Jeanette Weir, Marlene Winchester.

Extra special thanks to everyone who let me stay at their house and all the drivers that picked me up when I was hitchhiking. This book has been written on a shoe string budget. Being able to live for two months rent and travel free made this project achievable.

Biography

Jerry Vyse was born in 1988. His family have lived in the same house in the old part of Deal for four generations.

He achieved 3 A Levels from studying at Sandwich Technology School and Castle Community College. This has secured him a place at the University of Manchester to read Anthropology.

Prior to going to New Zealand, Jerry went on a coach trip from London to Sydney. The three month expedition went through twenty countries, including Iran, Pakistan and Burma. He is currently editing video footage of his travels into a feature film.

He funded his trip and this book through a variety of jobs - bar work, mail sorting, tour guiding, busking, toilet cleaning, labouring for builders and giving out change in a bingo hall.

This is his first book.

Jerry can be contacted by emailing:
thedealboatmen@hotmail.com